Magic is believing in yourself;
if you can do that, you can make anything happen.

—Johann Wolfgang von Goethe

For my children, Katherine, Alexander, and Christopher —E.D.

To my husband, who always celebrates my wins
and shrugs off my setbacks —V.T.K.

Anne Schwartz Books, an imprint of Random House Children's Books
A division of Penguin Random House LLC, 1745 Broadway, New York, NY 10019
penguinrandomhouse.com | rhcbooks.com

Editor: Anne Schwartz | Designer: Taline Boghosian | Copy Editor: Alison Kolani
Managing Editor: Emily Hoffman | Production Manager: Claribel Vasquez

Library of Congress Cataloging-in-Publication Data
Names: Duncan, Elizabeth, author. | Tentler-Krylov, Victoria, illustrator.
Title: Antonia and her magic wand / Elizabeth Duncan ; [illustrations by] Victoria Tentler-Krylov
Description: New York: Anne Schwartz Books, 2026. | Includes bibliographical references. | Audience: Ages 3–7
Summary: "This is a nonfiction picture book biography of Antonia Brico, the groundbreaking musician who defied convention to become one of the first women to conduct a world-class symphony orchestra" —Provided by publisher.
Identifiers: LCCN 2024001838 (print) | LCCN 2024001839 (ebook) | ISBN 978-0-593-81392-8 (hardcover)
ISBN 978-0-593-81393-5 (lib. bdg.) | ISBN 978-0-593-81394-2 (ebook)
Subjects: LCSH: Brico, Antonia—Juvenile literature. | Women conductors (Music)—United States—Biography—Juvenile literature.
Conductors (Music)—United States—Biography—Juvenile literature.
Classification: LCC ML3930.B8 D86 2026 (print) | LCC ML3930.B8 (ebook) | DDC 784.2092 [B]—dc23/eng/20240402

The text of this book is set in 14-point ABC Arizona Flare.
The art for this book was created using watercolor as well as Procreate and Adobe Photoshop.

Manufactured in China 10 9 8 7 6 5 4 3 2 1

The authorized representative in the EU for product safety and compliance is Penguin Random House Ireland, Morrison Chambers, 32 Nassau Street, Dublin D02 YH68, Ireland, https://eu-contact.penguin.ie.

Random House Children's Books supports the First Amendment and celebrates the right to read.

Antonia and Her Magic Wand

The Extraordinary Story of Antonia Brico, Symphony Conductor

written by
Elizabeth Duncan

illustrated by
Victoria Tentler-Krylov

a·s·b
anne schwartz books

YEAR
1908

Antonia listens to the music floating up to her window from the street below. There is no music in her California home. Only a chorus of rules about what little girls can't do. She aches for a melody of her own.

Silence . . .

loneliness . . .

sadness.

Antonia chews her fingernails. Her mother scolds and arranges piano lessons to stop her nervous habit.

Antonia's hands dance on piano keys, chasing away her sadness.

Music fills her, thrills her!

Notes and chords, melody and harmony, runs and trills. Ten small fingers working alone. But together they create magic. Her heart lifts for the first time.

Watching her first symphony concert, Antonia is spellbound. One hundred musicians, each with their own part, play with one voice. The conductor's baton dips and soars. Antonia realizes the whole orchestra is a single instrument, played by the conductor and his magic wand!

To conduct a symphony
is to make **magic.**

Surprise . . .
inspiration . . .
possibility.

When Antonia starts college to study piano, she enters an enchanted world! Music rings from rehearsal rooms, classrooms, and concert halls! She practices for hours upon hours.

As young men prepare to become professional musicians, most women prepare to become music teachers. But the magic wand has cast its spell, and Antonia dreams of conducting.

Secretly she studies whole symphonies.
She knows a conductor must
understand every instrument.

Her fingers move on violins and cellos.
Her breath fills oboes and tubas.
Her arms bang drums and crash cymbals.

The symphony builds inside
Antonia, instrument
upon instrument.

Antonia gets a job working for a conductor. She helps him organize his music and keeps things running smoothly during performances.

Finally, she makes her conducting dreams known. Her professors and fellow students laugh.

“Ladies are not allowed to play in symphonies!
And a woman conductor? Ridiculous!”

Antonia’s arms must stay at her side.
Her hands do not hold a baton.
She does not step onto a podium.

But Antonia won't take no for an answer. She moves to New York City to study with a great piano master.

Her days are filled with hours of piano practice, but she sneaks away at night to go to conducting classes. When her piano teacher finds out, he is furious and forbids her to attend.

LIST OF JOBS
THEATER ORCHESTRA

No matter where she goes or how hard she works, the doors remain shut. Antonia hears the same refrain: “You must stop this nonsense.” She tunes it out because she believes in the music within her.

Where can her symphony find a voice?

Antonia sets sail for Europe. She wants to attend the very best conducting school there—the Master School of Conducting at the Berlin State Academy of Music. But first she must be admitted, something no American and no woman has ever done before.

As waves beat against the ship,
Antonia's heart beats with purpose.

Courage . . . confidence . . . hope.

"You're from California? You're a girl?
You want to be a conductor?"
the German professor asks.

"Yes! Yes! And **YES!**"

Antonia auditions.
Eyebrows arch.

She takes their exams.
Heads nod.

She conducts a small
group of musicians. Smiles
peek through stern faces.

Antonia paces and waits. Will they accept her? Can they see all of her? The entire symphony that is Antonia?

Yes! Yes! And **YES!**

Antonia waves her conductor's baton. She discovers how to keep the beat and inspire musicians. She studies the composers' music until she understands every single note. She learns to control the chaos of twenty different parts, all playing at the same time.

When should the orchestra play loud or soft, sweet or bold?

How long should a note be held?

When is the exact moment all the musicians should come to a dramatic stop?

How should her body move to help the musicians feel the music?

It is the hardest thing Antonia has ever done.
And she loves every moment.

Finally, she is ready. The grand concert hall in Berlin buzzes with excitement. Antonia strides onto the stage.

She lifts her baton and
casts a musical spell.

As she conducts, she is the symphony. The magic flows from her heart and into her arms, to the tip of the wand, into the orchestra, and out into the world.

Preparation . . .

perseverance . . .

joy!

But just as Antonia reaches her dream,
the sounds of war drown out the music.

Antonia flees Germany and returns to America, where times are hard. She remembers how music filled her life with magic and hope. She longs to feel that hope again and share the magic with others.

But no professional symphony will hire
a woman conductor or even women
musicians. The door that Antonia cracked
open in Europe stays shut tight here.

Tired of being told what
she can’t do, she declares,
“If I can’t find an orchestra
to conduct, I’ll make my own!”

Bravura:
to play with daring
and brilliance

Antonia creates a brand-new orchestra, and eager musicians answer her call. The New York Women's Symphony Orchestra shows America what women can do. Sold-out crowds shout "Brava!" as Antonia conducts.

United . . .

passionate . . .

restless.

Antonia leads a protest demanding equal opportunities. "Professional orchestras should be open to everyone!" the chorus chants.

She is interviewed on the radio and profiled in concert programs. There are speeches, letters, and debates. Her name makes newspaper headlines.

Is her voice loud enough? Will the music world listen? Can they hear the symphony that is Antonia?

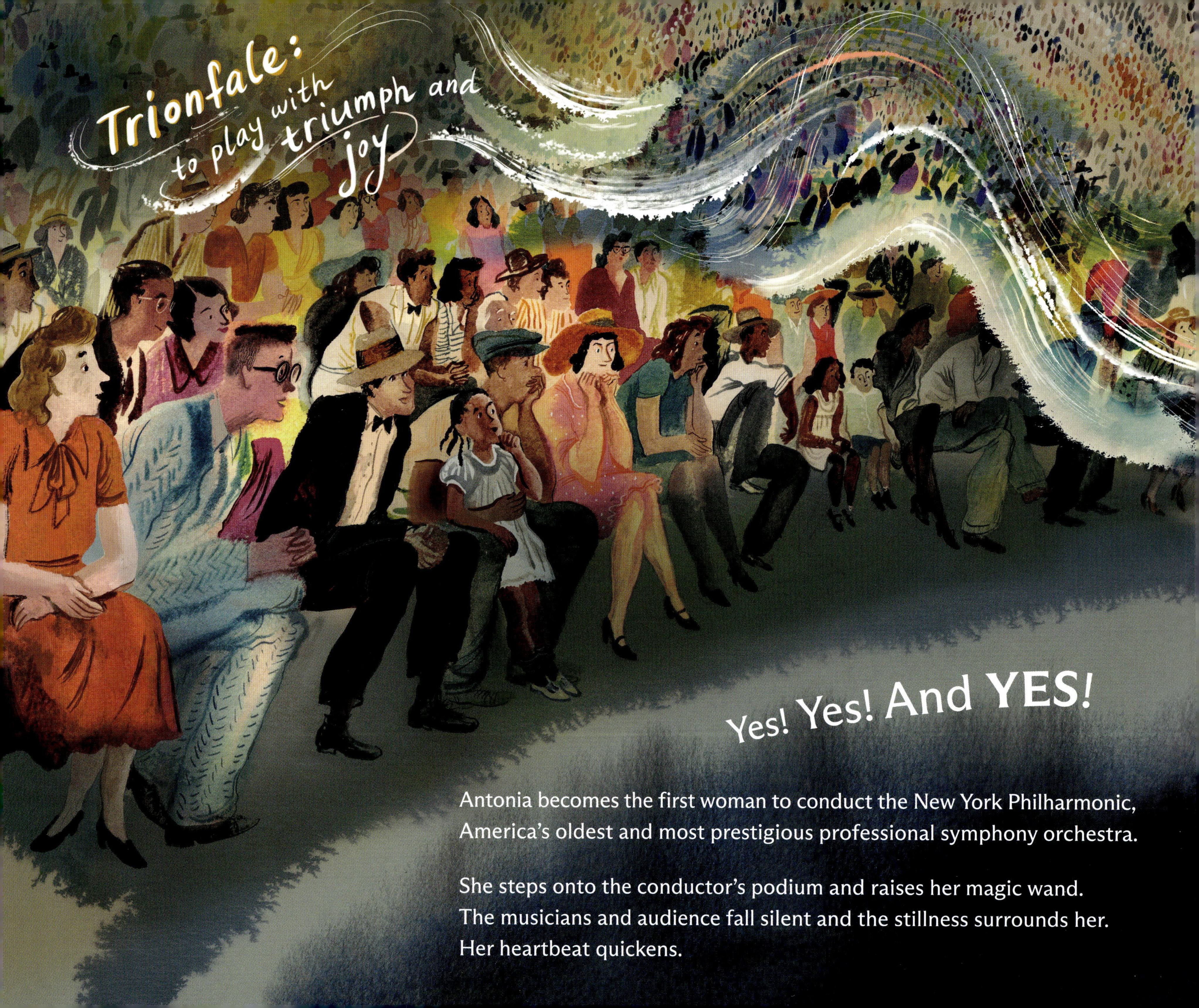

Yes! Yes! And YES!

Antonia becomes the first woman to conduct the New York Philharmonic, America's oldest and most prestigious professional symphony orchestra.

She steps onto the conductor's podium and raises her magic wand. The musicians and audience fall silent and the stillness surrounds her. Her heartbeat quickens.

She smiles. Swift and steady,
her baton signals the downbeat.

The magic begins.

More About Antonia

When I was a teenager studying the violin, my father surprised me with tickets to see Antonia Brico conducting her community symphony in Denver. I remember the thrill I felt as Dr. Brico strode onto the stage and began waving her baton. Her confidence and competence filled the small auditorium, and this experience stayed with me over the years. When I learned more about her story, I wanted the next generation of musical dreamers to follow their hearts and to be inspired by her.

Here's a little more information about this remarkable woman: Antonia Brico was born in 1902 in Rotterdam, Netherlands, to a single mother. Unable to care for Antonia, she put her in a foster home. Her foster parents moved to Oakland, California, when Antonia was still a baby and changed her name to Wilhelmina Wolhaus. She did not know the story of her birth until she was a teenager. At twenty-two years old, she changed her name back to Antonia Brico.

Antonia began playing the piano at age ten, and her first teacher was a young neighbor whose family owned a piano. By the time she was sixteen, Antonia was a master pianist.

Antonia attended the University of California, Berkeley, music program and worked to support herself. She demonstrated pianos in a music store and played popular songs to sell sheet music in a five-and-dime store.

While studying conducting in Germany, she reconnected with her birth family in the Netherlands. Although her mother had died, Antonia formed strong relationships with other relatives.

In 1938, the New York Philharmonic—the oldest and one of the best symphonies in America—invited Antonia to conduct a concert in New York City at their summer venue, the Lewisohn Stadium. She became the first woman in America to conduct the famous orchestra. Headlines around the country read "Music Barrier Falls! Woman Leads New York Symphony!" After the concert, Antonia was invited to guest-conduct orchestras all over the country.

Still, Antonia struggled the rest of her life with discrimination against women conductors. To her disappointment and frustration, she was never hired to be the permanent conductor of a professional symphony orchestra. She moved to Denver, Colorado, to audition to conduct the Denver Symphony, but the job went to a man.

In Denver, Antonia opened the Brico Music Studio, where she taught piano, conducting, and voice lessons. During the 1940s and 1950s, she traveled to Europe to guest-conduct world-class symphony orchestras. She continued her work with the musicians union, advocating for symphony members to be hired based on their musical ability.

In 1947, Antonia became the conductor of the Denver Businessmen's Orchestra, a semi-professional symphony. She led the orchestra for thirty-nine years. In 1968, it was renamed the Brico Symphony.

As time passed, Antonia lost her contacts in the world of symphonic music. Fewer and fewer guest-conducting opportunities were offered to her. Then, in 1974, one of her former piano students made a documentary called *Antonia: A Portrait of the Woman*, which told the story of Antonia's struggle with discrimination. It was nominated for an Academy Award and led to invitations for Antonia to conduct major symphonies all over America and abroad.

Antonia died in 1989, at the age of 87.

Women Musicians and Conductors Today

Today, if you go to a symphony concert, you will see many women musicians. But until the 1960s, women in the United States were not allowed to play in professional orchestras, except for the occasional harpist.

Through the work of Antonia Brico and others, the rules against women musicians started to change. In the late 1960s, orchestras began to have "blind auditions," in which people tried out for an orchestra hidden behind a screen. The screen let the jurors focus on the quality of the music, rather than the appearance of the musician. As a result, women musicians in American orchestras increased from 6 percent in 1970 to almost 50 percent in 2022.

But women conductors remain very rare. A blind audition is, of course, impossible for a symphony conductor. Until recently, only one woman, Marin Alsop, had risen to lead a major symphony. Then, in 2022, the Atlanta Symphony Orchestra hired Nathalie Stutzmann to conduct. Antonia's determination and successes are an example for a new generation of musicians as they reach for their dreams.

Bibliography

Antonia Brico Collection. History Colorado, Stephen H. Hart Research Center. Collection includes newspaper clippings, interviews, and speeches.

Antonia Brico Papers. Denver Public Library, Western History and Genealogy. Collection includes newspaper clippings, interviews, speeches, program notes, concert reviews, and annotated scrapbooks with programs. https://archives.denverlibrary.org/repositories/3/resources/6019

Christensen, Lance Eugene. "'I Will Not Be Deflected from My Course': The Life of Dr. Antonia Brico." MA thesis, University of Colorado–Denver, 2000.

Collins, Judy, and Jill Godmilow, dirs. *Antonia: A Portrait of the Woman.* Momentum Pictures, 1974.

Katsarelis, Cynthia, Musical Director and Conductor, Pro Musica Colorado Chamber Orchestra, interview, February 2022.

Quotations

"Ladies are not allowed . . .": Dr. Antonia Brico, interviewed by Judy Collins, *Antonia: A Portrait of the Woman*, 1974, compiled quotes.

"You're from California . . .": Dr. Antonia Brico, transcript of lecture titled "One Undeflected Step at a Time," April 14, 1975 (Antonia Brico Papers, Denver Public Library).

"If I can't find an orchestra . . .": Dr. Antonia Brico, interviewed by Judy Collins, *Antonia: A Portrait of the Woman*, 1974.

"Professional orchestras . . . ," "Women Urge Equal Rights": *The New York Times*, May 19, 1938 (Antonia Brico Papers, Denver Public Library).